PANCAKES, CRÊPES & WAFFLES

PANCAKES, CRÊPES & WAFFLES

Martha Lomask

PIATKUS

© 1983 Martha Lomask

First published in 1983 by
Judy Piatkus (Publishers) Limited
of Loughton, Essex

British Library Cataloguing in Publication Data
Lomask, Martha
    Pancakes, crepes & waffles
    1. Pancakes, waffles, etc.
    I. Title
    641.8   TX745
    ISBN 0-86188-200-8

Design and artwork by Paul Saunders
Jacket designed by Ken Leeder

Typeset by Phoenix Photosetting, Chatham
Printed and bound by Mackays of Chatham Ltd

Contents

Introduction

Pancakes in some form – thin as a leaf or thick and robust – are among the oldest forms of bread in the world. Ground or pounded grain mixed with water could be baked on any flat heated rock, long before bake-ovens were thought of. The unleavened bread of Biblical times is probably a kind of pancake. And the sophisticated Chinese seem to have been making their egg-roll pancakes for nearly 3,000 years. Every type of grain has been, and is still being, used to make this universally loved food: wheat, oats, barley, cornmeal or maize, rice and buckwheat, among others.

'Pancake' to the English usually means a thin rollable affair, made from a rather rich batter not unlike that used for Yorkshire pudding. It is, of course, a cross-channel version of the European crêpe – which is often misleadingly called a pancake in English too! True crêpes are always very thin, delicate, and quickly made in a small hot pan. 'Pancake' to North Americans means something quite different: a thick and hearty griddle cake, usually served for breakfast with syrup, bacon or sausages, and lashings of coffee. An American pancake is rather like a drop scone or Scotch pancake.

Astonishingly, crêpes and pancakes are far easier to make than is usually thought, and are always greeted with gratifying applause far out of proportion to the effort that goes into them.

Anything more versatile than a thin pancake or crêpe would be hard to find. It can be made small, about 5 inches (13 cm) across, or literally as big as a dinner plate and served with nothing more than a gloss of butter, a squeeze of lemon and some sugar, or wrapping an infinite number of fillings sweet or savoury.

All pancakes, paper-thin or robust, are chameleons: appearing now as chapattis with curry, next day as a tortilla with Mexican food. They can be served spectacularly with a flaming French sauce, or in a very plebian way filled with jam and eaten with the fingers. Try them deep-fried, baked, rolled or stacked, hot or cold. A good cook of my acquaintance describes them as 'very forgiving' food, because they are agreeable to being cooked long in advance, stored, frozen, and reheated.

Waffles, the kissing cousin of pancakes, are thought to go back to the fourteenth century. The name comes from the old High German word meaning both 'honeycomb' and 'weave', descriptive of the deeply-indented surface. Together with the beautiful patterned irons, the word passed into Flemish and French as *waffre*, then finally evolved into *gauffre* in European languages, while staying close to its original in English.

Waffles are very nearly as versatile as crêpes and pancakes, although they cannot be rolled. In Britain, they are quickly gaining in popularity and are most often served as a rather super breakfast or brunch dish. In the United States and Canada, they go far beyond that and are often used as the basis for supper dishes made with delicious savoury mixtures.

Batters

All crêpes, pancakes and waffles are based on egg, flour and some kind of liquid, which can be water, milk, buttermilk, yoghurt, beer or orange juice. Sometimes a raising agent is added, and sometimes there is a small amount of melted butter or oil in the mixture.

I am often asked about making crêpe and pancake batter in blenders and food processors. Much as I love my miracle machines, I do not use them for this. Over-mixing makes batter tough, and it is hard to control the time and speed of these super-powerful super-quick pieces of equipment. Making batter in a bowl with a sturdy spoon or hand whisk is only á matter of two or three minutes and there is no danger of over-beating.

Flours

The range of flours for pancake- and waffle-making is unlimited. I have used everything from everyday supermarket white to various brown flours, rye, buckwheat and cornmeal. I must confess here to personal preference: every recipe in this book has been made both with plain white flour and with 'Country Cookbook' self-raising light brown flour (Jordan's), and of the two I prefer the flavour and texture of the latter. But remember this: once you have filled, rolled, or stacked whatever crêpe, pancake or waffle you make, *no one will ever know the difference*. The slight amount of raising agent in self-raising flours does not affect the performance one whit.

Measurements

Throughout, recipes are set out in both Imperial and metric measures – please, *please* use one or the other, but do not mix them.

Teaspoons and tablespoons are from a standard Imperial set. But if you have invested in a metric set, the *rough* equivalents are:

1 tablespoon=15 ml spoon
1 teaspoon = 5 ml spoon
½ teaspoon = 2 ml spoon

All spoon measurements are level, unless otherwise stated. But don't worry about it! You are not dealing with gold dust but with measures of butter, sugar, yoghurt, milk, and various flours – a little more or a little less is not going to affect the end result in the least.

Freezing

Pancakes, crêpes and waffles all freeze well, but I have to confess that as far as the first two are concerned, I seldom do it. It is so incredibly easy and quick to prepare them from the beginning, that I would rather make them fresh each time than wait for them to thaw. My invaluable Universal Pancake Mix (page 56), kept in an air-tight jar, makes it possible to turn out enough hearty pancakes for four stalwart breakfast-eaters in about 15 minutes. Crêpe batter, unless you are surrounded by utter purists, can be made almost instantly and cooked up without the traditional wait-and-rest period. Twelve to eighteen crêpes can be ready, from batter-mixing to rolling and saucing, in about 12 minutes once you are past the novice stage.

However, if you do want to freeze, cool the crêpes or pancakes and assemble them in stacks with a round of greaseproof paper separating each. Overwrap in freezer wrap or foil, seal, label and date, and freeze them for up to 3 months. Bring back to room temperature before trying to peel them apart.

Crêpes are delicate and their nice lacy brown edges break at a touch when frozen. I find it best to put the wrapped stack in a suitable-sized plastic container to keep neighbouring frozen packages from knocking them around. A friend freezes hers between two round foil plates taped together, which is a very good idea.

Frozen *filled* crêpes I find very tricky because domestic freezers, unlike commercial blast-freezing, simply do not work fast enough to keep a rich or creamy filling from soaking into the thin crêpe. I can only say, *experiment*. Why not freeze the filling in appropriate quantities, and thaw to roll up in freshly-made crêpes? If you do want to freeze rolled and filled ones, wrap each separately, open-freeze on a baking sheet, then carefully pack them together in a plastic container or foil bag like so many little logs.

Waffles, however, are something else again. Because they take so much longer to bake than pancakes (from 5 to 8 minutes) you can find yourself standing over the iron, temper fraying, while everyone else wolfs them up. Make them in advance, and refrigerate, absolutely flat and tightly wrapped; or freeze, individually wrapped and *flat*. Whisk them out, slip them still frozen into your toaster (or under the grill), and they are as good as or better than freshly-made. They burn rather easily, so watch the temperature.

It is pointless to freeze pancake or crêpe batter since it is so easy to make. But you *can* refrigerate it for up to 24 hours, tightly sealed in a bowl or jug. It will separate, it will probably thicken, and it will turn a horrid greyish colour. Stir it well, thin with water or milk, and don't attempt to keep any left-over batter after this procedure as it ferments easily.

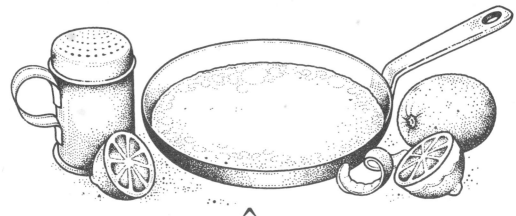

CRÊPES

Of all the dishes in the world, perhaps only a towering soufflé calls forth as much praise (and envy) as successful crêpes. Yet when you say, truthfully, 'They're so easy', you get an unfair amount of credit for modesty. Talk about having your crêpe and eating it too! The making of crêpes, curiously enough, seems to terrify even some very good cooks. It is hard to believe that they are so incredibly simple to make: that a tissue-thin crêpe cooks to perfection in less than a minute, and despite its delicate look is strong enough to stand up to freezing, for days, weeks, even months. And crêpes turn even the most mundane left-overs into something always interesting, often delectable.

Dessert crêpes are a truly superb way of making a not-very-interesting meal into something memorable. Think how delicious the simple Jaffa Pancakes (page 36) would be after plain grilled chops and a salad. All the ingredients (crêpes and filling) can be made hours or days in advance, and flung together with a fine flourish in only about three or four minutes. Even the showiest creations take only a few minutes to finish off.

Don't limit yourself to conventional rolling, folding and stacking. Why not try deep-fried crêpes – crusty and dry on the outside, with a burst of flavour inside?

Or bake crêpes crisp over patty tins and fill with any sweet or savoury mixture. Cut them in strips or squares, sprinkle with a zesty topping, bake in the oven and serve with drinks. Snip crêpes into narrow oblongs and drop into simmering clear soup, instead of croûtons. Turn them into Indian Samosas, Chinese Spring Rolls or American-Jewish Blintzes.

Crêpes are not only beautifully versatile, but are almost impossible to get wrong – if they're not perfectly round, perfectly smooth, perfectly coloured, no matter. When they are filled or sauced, rolled or stacked or grilled or flamed, who's to know? If a tiny hole appears in the cooking, patch it with a drop of batter and all is well. And no one ever gets bored with crêpes! (I speak as one who has lived with them in all their varieties, meal after meal for months on end, and still long to try still another variation.)

Crêpe Pans

The classic French pans are steel, with a sharply angled side that stops the crêpe batter from running up. They may be any size from 4 inches (10 cm) to about 9 inches (15 cm). They rust, and the handles get hot.

An omelette pan with its slightly rounded sides makes perfect crêpes, I find. There's a deal of nonsense written about what kind of crêpe pan you *must* have – pay no attention. Non-stick, enamel, cast iron, steel, use what gives you the best results. And truly, you don't have to keep one pan sacred, wiped out and never washed, for making crêpes and only crêpes. Some of my best ones are made in an eighteen-year-old, fairly lightweight, non-stick 7 inch (18 cm) omelette pan with a neatly ridged, plastic-covered handle that comes sweetly to my hand. It is used by everyone in the family for omelettes, scrambled eggs, fried eggs, *croque monsieur.* However, it is *never* assaulted with steel or aluminium forks or spoons, nor cleaned with scouring powder or metal pads. The surface is like silk satin. For big 8–9 inch (20–23 cm) crêpes, the shallow Tefal non-stick pancake pan is excellent.

I use a fairly wide, and rather expensive, Teflon-coated palette knife for loosening crêpes – cheaper ones, exposed to the heat of the pan, develop nibbled edges.

Let your crêpe pan cool down before washing it, and treat it like fine china, cleaning it with a dishbrush, detergent or soap flakes. Dry it well, and store it where the surface cannot be scored by carelessly-stacked pans.

Master Directions

1. Mix the batter until all the flour has disappeared, but do not over-beat as this makes tough little rounds of leather. Let it rest, if you have time, for about 2 hours to expand the gluten in the flour. The batter should be only of the thickness of single cream. If it has thick-ened, thin it cautiously with water, not milk.

2. Crêpe pans must be silk-smooth to the touch. Try not to use them for frying meat or vegetables which get vigorous stirring.

3. Heat the pan on moderate heat until drops of cold water dance and bounce on the surface. If the water vanishes, it's too hot. If it steams sullenly, it's too cool. You will need to adjust the heat under your pan, fractionally up and down, throughout the cooking process – each pouring of the batter slightly alters the surface temperature.

4. Very, very lightly brush the pan with a folded pad of kitchen paper which has been dabbed in a *little* oil. The surface must look like very expensive dull satin, not shiny rayon. Keep watching it: some crêpe batters have little or no fat in the mixture, so you must *lightly* brush the pan between every two or three crêpes. Greasy pans give you crêpes that slide out evenly and can be flipped high and over – this is spectacular, but the crêpes are not very nice. Non-stick pans need an almost invisible film of oil.

5. A 6–7 inch (15–18 cm) crêpe needs about 3 tablespoons of batter. Find yourself a small ladle or, better still, a little after-dinner coffee cup which, half-filled, will pour out the right quantity. By the time you have made your first six or eight crêpes, you will find that you can judge the amount to perfection.

6. Raise the pan from the heat with one hand, pour the batter into the centre very quickly and turn and swirl it so that a thin film rolls around and 'seizes'. Put the pan back on the heat. If there are a few little holes, drop in a little batter from a spoon to fill them. Don't worry about edges, you can always trim.

7. Cook for about 30–40 seconds, raise one edge with your palette knife and if it is smooth and golden brown loosen the entire crêpe. Grasp the edge near you in your fingers, pull it up sharply and flip it over. The second side takes only about 15 seconds to cook. It will be speckly, not elegantly smooth.

8. Stack the crêpes, separated by wide strips of greaseproof paper or foil, on a warm plate, and cover with an inverted plate. If you are going to use them at once, set the plate above a saucepan of simmering water or keep them in a very cool oven (200°F/100°C/Gas ¼). If you plan to fill and roll them, lay them out speckled-side up; if they are to be layered, the golden-smooth side should be uppermost.

9. To reheat crêpes, heat the oven to 325°F/165°C/Gas 3. Lay the crêpes in one layer on a baking sheet and cover with a loose tent of foil and heat for about 10 minutes. Alternatively, stack them, separated with foil pieces, on a plate, cover with a bowl or inverted plate and heat over a saucepan of simmering water.

The Simplest Crêpe

Makes about 21 crêpes, 6 inches (15 cm) across

This is a French recipe which flies in the face of the tradition that says crêpe batter must contain melted butter, brandy, extra egg yolks, and must stand for hours before cooking. It can be refrigerated for up to 3 days, but must be well-stirred and perhaps thinned with a little water before cooking. Don't be alarmed at the greyish, unhealthy look of the stored batter – that's normal. These crêpes can be filled with any sweet or savoury mixture.

3 eggs, size 3
3 oz (75 g) white or 85% flour
8 fl oz (225 ml) milk, or half milk and half water

1. Whisk together the egg and flour, gradually stir in the liquid and mix until fairly smooth. A few tiny lumps don't matter. Do not over-beat. The batter should be like single cream.
2. Cook as in the Master Directions, pages 12–13. This is a thin, rich, delicate crêpe and must be carefully loosened from the pan when you turn it.

Wholewheat Crêpes

Makes about 20 crêpes, 6 inches (15 cm) across

These wholewheat *thin* pancakes are not to be confused with what in Canada and the United States are called Wheatcakes or Stack of Wheats – thick, soft pancakes served for breakfast. Fill these crêpes with any savoury creamed mixture and heat through for about 15 minutes in the oven at 300°F/150°C/Gas 2.

2 oz (50 g) wholewheat flour
2 oz (50 g) 85% flour
1 oz (25 g) dry milk powder
1 teaspoon salt
4 eggs, size 3 or 4
8 fl oz (225 ml) milk
1 tablespoon vegetable oil

1. Sift the dry ingredients into a bowl. Beat the eggs with the milk and oil and gradually stir into the dry ingredients. Mix well, but do not over-beat. Do not make this batter in a blender as it will cause the crêpes to be tough.
2. Cook as in Master Directions, pages 12–13. Between making each crêpe, stir the batter and very lightly grease the pan with oil so that it glistens dully.

French Light Pancakes

Makes about 16 crêpes, 5 inches (13 cm) across

These pancakes are known in France as Crêpes Légères. They are light and airy, not meant to be rolled, but to be dusted with icing sugar and eaten at once. Or roll into a cone-shape, drop in about a teaspoon of good jam, and eat from the hand.

5 oz (150 g) white flour
5 fl oz (150 ml) milk
5 fl oz (150 ml) lukewarm water
2 oz (50 g) butter or margarine, melted
pinch of salt
2 eggs, size 2, separated
rind of half a lemon, grated
icing sugar

1. Mix the flour with the milk and water and stir until smooth, but do not over-beat. Add 1 tablespoon of the melted butter or margarine and the salt. Cover and let it stand about an hour.
2. Beat the egg yolks with the remaining butter and the lemon rind, and in a large bowl whisk the egg whites to stiff peaks. Pour the egg yolk mixture on top of the whites and fold together. Gently stir in the batter and mix lightly.
3. Drop by heaped tablespoonfuls on a lightly greased crêpe pan, and spread slightly with the spoon to make rounds of about 5 inches (13 cm). Cook until the bottom is golden and the top beginning to look dry, turn and cook on the other side. Dust with icing sugar.

English Pancakes

Makes about 12 crêpes, 5 inches (13 cm) across

These are traditional for Pancake Day – slightly heavier than the classic very thin French crêpes – and always served with lemon and sugar.

4 oz (100 g) white flour
pinch of salt
1 egg, size 3
5 fl oz (150 ml) milk
5 fl oz (150 ml) water
1 teaspoon vegetable oil
about 1 tablespoon melted lard
caster sugar
lemon juice
lemon wedges

1. Sift the flour and salt together into a basin, make a well in the centre and break in the egg. Add a little milk and stir gently. Add the rest of the milk slowly and stir until smooth. Stir in the water and oil and beat for 1 minute. Cover and let the batter stand for 1 hour. Stir.

2. Melt a little lard in a crêpe or omelette pan and when it bubbles, pour in about 2 tablespoonfuls of the batter. Cook as in Master Directions, pages 12–13.

3. Slide each pancake out on to a piece of sugared greaseproof paper on a heated plate, and sprinkle with more sugar. Stack the pancakes. When all are cooked, sprinkle each with a little lemon juice, roll, and serve with more caster sugar and lemon wedges.

Blender-made Sweet Crêpes

Makes about 16 crêpes, 5 inches (13 cm) across

This is the best recipe I know for dessert crêpes made in a blender or food processor – in about 15 seconds you have a velvet-smooth batter, and the crêpes are not tough despite all that has been said about not over-beating. The crêpes are thin and delicate, so loosen them very carefully from the pan and pull up with your fingers to avoid tearing. They freeze successfully.

3 egg yolks, size 3
1 tablespoon caster sugar
3 tablespoons brandy or rum
½ teaspoon grated lemon or orange rind
6 fl oz (175 ml) milk
6 fl oz (175 ml) water
about 6 oz (175 g) white flour, sifted
generous 2 oz (50 g) butter or margarine, melted

1. Mix the egg yolks, sugar, brandy, grated rind, milk and water in the blender, then add the flour and melted butter and blend until smooth. Let the batter stand, covered, in a cool place for 2 hours. Stir well.
2. Bake as in Master Directions, pages 12–13.

Chocolate Crêpes

Makes about 18 crêpes, 6 inches (15 cm) across

These crêpes can be made up to 8 hours before serving, but they don't freeze well. The batter may be prepared and stored, covered, for up to 18 hours. They are delicious eaten on their own, sprinkled with caster sugar, or served with a generous helping of whipped cream.

1 oz (25 g) butter or good margarine
1 oz (25 g) plain dark chocolate
4 fl oz (100 ml) milk
5 fl oz (150 ml) water
2 eggs, size 3
4 oz (100 g) white or 85% flour

1. Melt the butter with the chocolate in a bowl set over simmering water. Beat the milk, water and eggs together and gradually stir into the flour. Add the chocolate butter and let the batter rest for 2 hours.
2. Cook as in Master Directions, pages 12–13. You will probably not need to oil the pan between crêpes, but watch it as you go.

Orange Pancakes

Makes about 12–16 pancakes, 6–7 inches (15–18 cm) across

This recipe came to me from Israel by way of California, and it lends itself to every possible variation with citrus sauces or spreads. Try grated orange rind beaten into butter as a topping, or serve with whipped butter (page 92).

8 oz (225 g) white or 85% flour
½ teaspoon bicarbonate of soda
½ teaspoon salt
1–2 eggs, size 3
2 fl oz (50 ml) vegetable oil
about 12 fl oz (350 ml) orange juice

1. Sift the dry ingredients into a large bowl. Whisk the eggs and oil together and slowly stir into the flour mixture. Mix well, and gradually pour in enough orange juice to make a batter of the thickness of single cream.
2. Cook as in Master Directions, pages 12–13. Serve at once, spread with very cold unsalted butter, for a luxurious breakfast, or as Jaffa Pancakes (page 36) for a dessert.

Crêpes D'Aligre

Serves 6 as a starter, or 3 as a luncheon dish

Very rich – and I'm sorry, but it really cannot be made with anything less extravagant than shrimps, mayonnaise and whipped cream!

**12 crêpes, 7 inches (18 cm) across
(recipes pages 14 and 15)**

**6 oz (175 g) peeled shrimps
2 teaspoons lemon juice
½ teaspoon Worcestershire sauce
2 generous tablespoons mayonnaise
2 generous tablespoons chopped chives
2 generous tablespoons whipped cream
5 fl oz (125 ml) single cream
1 generous tablespoon grated Parmesan cheese**

Preheat the oven to 350°F/180°C/Gas 4.
1. Mix together the shrimps, lemon juice and Worcestershire sauce and put some of the mixture in the centre of each crêpe. Lightly mix the mayonnaise with 1 tablespoon of chives and the whipped cream, and spoon over the shrimp mixture. Roll the crêpes and put them, seam-side down, in a buttered shallow baking dish.
2. Stir the remaining chives into the single cream, pour over the pancakes and sprinkle with Parmesan. Bake for about 15 minutes until the cheese begins to turn golden. Serve at once.

Smoked Salmon Crêpes

Serves 4 as a starter

Smoked salmon scraps are often available cheaply in the delicatessen department of supermarkets so even with the Hollandaise this lovely starter isn't as costly as it sounds and tastes. You can buy the sauce or make your own.

8 crêpes, 6–7 inches (15–18 cm) across
(recipes pages 14 and 15)

4–6 oz (100–175 g) smoked salmon trimmings
3 hard boiled eggs, size 3
2 oz (50 g) butter
1 teaspoon finely chopped dillweed
6 fl oz (175 ml) Hollandaise sauce

Preheat the oven to 350°F/180°C/Gas 4.
1. Mince together (or blend in food processor or blender) the salmon, eggs, 1 oz (25 g) of the butter and the dill. Spoon the filling in a line down the centre of each crêpe and roll up. Put them, seam-side down, in a shallow ovenproof dish.
2. Cut the remaining butter in flakes over the crêpes and bake in the centre of the oven for 10 minutes. Mask the crêpes with the Hollandaise and put the dish near the top of the oven. Bake for a further 5 minutes until the sauce bubbles. Serve at once.

Mushroom Crêpes

Serves 4 to 6

These heavenly little bundles may be served as a starter, or as a vegetable with some plainly-cooked meat – and they are best served not too
hot and dusted with chopped parsley.

**12 crêpes, 7 inches (18 cm) across
(recipes pages 14 and 15, reserving about 2 tablespoons of batter)**

**4 oz (100 g) butter or margarine
1 tablespoon oil
1 small onion, finely chopped
1 lb (450 g) mushrooms, wiped and diced
½ teaspoon dried tarragon, or 1 teaspoon fresh chopped tarragon
½ teaspoon salt
freshly ground black pepper
2 eggs, size 3
4 oz (100 g) fine dry breadcrumbs**

1. Heat 2 oz (50 g) of the butter and a little oil and gently cook the onion
until it is soft and limp. Stir in the mushrooms and cook for about 15
minutes, until they begin to look dry. Add tarragon, salt and pepper.
2. Put about 1 tablespoon of the mixture in the centre of each crêpe.
Turn in the top and bottom, then fold in the sides and seal with a dab of
batter. Lay them seam-side down on a plate.
3. When needed, lightly beat the eggs, dip in each crêpe, then carefully
turn over in the breadcrumbs. Heat the remaining butter and oil in a
large shallow frying pan, and gently fry the crêpes on each side.

Turkey Blintzes

Serves 8 as a starter, 4 as a main dish

This recipe can be prepared in advance to Stage 2 and refrigerated.

8 crêpes, 7 inches (18 cm) across
(recipes pages 14 and 15)

8 oz (225 g) cooked turkey breast, diced
4 oz (100 g) Emmenthal, German Loaf or Gouda cheese, diced
5 fl oz (150 ml) thick Béchamel or white sauce, cooled
small pinch of grated nutmeg
1 teaspoon dry white wine or dry sherry
1 tablespoon grated Parmesan cheese (optional)
1 egg, size 1 or 2, separated
2 tablespoons water
pinch of salt
flour
3–4 oz (75–100 g) fine dry light brown breadcrumbs
oil for deep frying   lemon wedges

1. Mix the turkey and cheese with the sauce. Stir in the nutmeg, wine and Parmesan. Put a spoonful in the centre of each crêpe. Fold the bottom and top in, and the sides over, then seal with a little egg white.
2. Whisk the remaining egg white and yolk together with the water and salt. Gently roll the filled crêpes in flour, egg, and then in breadcrumbs.
3. Heat the oil to 360°F/185°C. Fry two or three pancakes at a time until just golden. Drain on kitchen paper, and keep warm on a paper-lined baking tin in the oven. Serve garnished with lemon wedges.

Cheese Soufflé Crêpes

Serves 8 as a starter, 4 as a main course

Any soufflé-filled crêpe is tricky to bring off, but looks and tastes wonderful. Practise on your nearest and dearest.

16 crêpes, 6–7 inches (15–18 cm) across
(recipes pages 14 and 15)

4 eggs, size 3, separated
15 fl oz (425 ml) hot Béchamel or white sauce
2 oz (50 g) mild Cheddar or Double Gloucester cheese, grated
salt
freshly ground black pepper
pinch of cayenne
freshly grated nutmeg

Preheat the oven to 400°F/200°C/Gas 6.
1. Whisk the egg yolks lightly and stir in 2 tablespoons of the hot sauce. Mix, then stir back into the sauce on a very low heat. Add the cheese and mix well. Remove from the heat.
2. In a large bowl, whisk the egg whites to stiff peaks and stir 2 table-spoons into the cheese sauce to lighten it, mixing well. Scrape the sauce on to the rest of the egg whites and cut and fold together.
3. With the speckled side of each crêpe uppermost, put 1 heaped table-spoon of the cheese soufflé mixture on one half of each crepe and fold the other half over. Lay the crêpes in a buttered baking dish and bake for about 15 minutes until brown and puffy. Serve at once.

Chinese Egg Roll Pancakes

Makes 24–30

These egg rolls are fiddly to make but once you have conquered the problem of making the 'skins' thin enough to read through you are more than halfway home. They are not quite, but very nearly, like the very crisp ones you get in a Chinese restaurant. The filling may be varied to taste.

BATTER
3 eggs, size 3
scant 3½–4 oz (85–100 g) plain white flour
2 tablespoons cornflour
16–18 fl oz (450–500 ml) cold water
½ teaspoon salt

FILLING
1 generous tablespoon oil
6 oz (176 g) lean pork, finely chopped
4 oz (100 g) cooked shrimps or prawns, chopped
1 carrot, shredded
4 leaves Chinese cabbage, finely chopped
4 oz (100 g) mushrooms, wiped and finely chopped
2 stalks celery, finely chopped
8 water chestnuts (tinned), chopped
1 tablespoon soy sauce
2 tablespoons chopped spring onion
1 egg
½ teaspoon caster sugar

1. Whisk the eggs, beat in the flour, cornflour, water and salt. Mix very well (in a blender or food processor if you like). The batter should be very thin, like milk. Heat a 7–8 inch (18–20 cm) omelette or crêpe pan as in Master Directions, pages 12–13, and lightly grease it.

2. Take pan off heat, and pour in about 1 to 1½ tablespoons of the batter, tilting and swirling it very quickly. The pancake will be very, very thin. Set it back on moderate heat and cook only until the surface looks slightly dry and the edges curl up – the underside must not be at all brown. Cook on one side only. Gently loosen and slip out on a large sheet of doubled kitchen paper. Reserve about 2 tablespoons of batter for stage 4. When all pancakes are cooked, turn them over and fill the uncooked side. (They may also be kept stacked under a sheet of greaseproof paper with a damp towel laid over them until you want to fill them.)

3. To make the filling: heat the oil and sauté the pork with the shrimp for about 5 minutes. Add the vegetables and stir-fry about 2 minutes. Add the soy sauce, spring onion, egg and sugar and mix well. Cool.

4. Put about 1½ tablespoons of the mixture in the centre of each skin. Turn the bottom up and the sides in and seal the top with reserved batter. Lay the filled egg rolls on greaseproof paper and cover lightly with a damp cloth.

5. Heat the oil to 360°F/185°C in a deep-fryer. Fry the egg rolls, a few at a time, for about 3 to 4 minutes. Drain and keep hot.

Samosa Pancakes

Serves 4 to 6 as a snack or starter

Samosas may also be made with a spiced meat and vegetable filling.

**10–12 crêpes, 8 inches (20 cm) across
(recipes pages 14 and 15, reserving 2 tablespoons batter)**

**8 oz (225 g) chopped mixed vegetables (carrots, celery, onion, bean
sprouts, mild or hot red peppers, cauliflower florets)
a little crushed garlic
1 teaspoon mild or hot curry powder
½ teaspoon ground coriander
1 teaspoon flour
2 tablespoons mango chutney
salt and pepper
5 fl oz (150 ml) water or stock
oil for deep frying**

1. Lay out the crêpes, speckled side up, and cut each in half.
2. Heat the oil and stir-fry the vegetables and garlic for 5 minutes. Stir in
the curry powder, coriander and flour. Mix well, then add the water.
Simmer for 5 minutes, then add the chutney, salt and pepper.
3. Put a heaped tablespoon of filling in the centre of each crêpe. Dab
reserved batter around the inside edge of the crêpes, fold the curved
edge down and press firmly, then fold in the outer edges and seal.
4. Heat the oil to 375°F/190°C and deep fry the samosas a few at a time
until crisp and brown. Drain well. Keep hot on kitchen paper in the oven.

Florentine Fish Crêpes

Serves 4

A very economical and quick recipe that tastes rather luxurious.

8 crêpes, 7 inches (18 cm) across
(recipes pages 14 and 15)

4 oz (100 g) butter or margarine
2 rounded tablespoons plain flour
10 fl oz (275 ml) milk
salt and pepper
freshly grated nutmeg
4 oz (100 g) Cheddar cheese, grated
6 oz (175 g) cooked smoked haddock fillets, flaked
1 small onion, finely chopped
6 oz (175 g) frozen spinach, cooked and well drained

Preheat the oven to 400°F/200°C/Gas 6.
1. Mix 2 oz (50 g) of the butter, the flour, milk, salt, pepper and nutmeg in a large heavy saucepan and cook, stirring, on a moderate heat until boiling. Lower the heat and cook until the sauce is thick and smooth. Stir in 3 oz (75 g) cheese.
2. Heat 1 oz (25 g) of the butter in a frying pan and cook the onion until soft. Mix the onion with the fish, add the spinach and lightly stir into the sauce.
3. Put about 2 level tablespoons of filling on each crêpe, roll and put seam-side down in a buttered baking dish. Cut the remaining butter over the top and sprinkle with the cheese. Bake for about 10 minutes.

Chive Crêpes with Chicken and Mushrooms

Serves 4

This is a super way to make a light supper dish from cooked chicken.

**12 crêpes, 6–7 inches (15–18 cm) across
(recipes pages 14 and 15, adding 2 heaped tablespoons chopped fresh
or freeze-dried chives to the batter)**

**generous 1 oz (25 g) butter or margarine
10 oz (275 g) mushrooms, wiped and diced
5 oz (150 g) cooked chicken, diced
good pinch of freshly grated nutmeg
salt   freshly ground black pepper
1 tablespoon lemon juice
10 fl oz (275 ml) thick white sauce**

Preheat the oven to 350°F/180°C/Gas 4.
1. Heat the butter in a heavy frying pan and gently cook the mushrooms for about 5 minutes, stirring occasionally, until some of the moisture vanishes. Add the chicken and cook, stirring, for another minute. Season to taste with nutmeg, salt and pepper and stir in the lemon juice.
2. Mix a scant half of the white sauce into the chicken mixture. Spoon about 2 tablespoons of filling down the centre of each crêpe, roll and put seam-side down in a buttered baking dish. Pour over the remaining sauce and bake for about 15 minutes until heated through.

Savoury Crêpe Cheesecake

Serves 6 as a luncheon dish

A very nice, simple, easily-made dish which is rather like an Italian quiche. It is fairly rich, so servings can be small.

8 crêpes, 6–7 inches (15–18 cm) across
(recipes pages 14 and 15)

1 oz (25 g) butter or margarine with a little oil
4 oz (100 g) mushrooms, wiped and sliced
12 oz (350 g) curd or cream cheese
3 eggs, size 3
salt   freshly ground black pepper
4 oz (100 g) cooked ham, coarsely chopped
3 oz (75 g) tinned sweet red pimentos

Preheat oven to 350°F/180°C/Gas 4.
1. Line a round or oval casserole or quiche dish with the crêpes, over-lapping them. Heat the butter and oil in a frying pan and sauté the mushrooms for about 3 minutes. Whisk the curd cheese, eggs and sea-soning in a bowl and stir in the ham and sautéed mushrooms.
2. Pour the filling into the crêpe-lined dish. Cut the pimentos into even-sized pieces and lay them around the edge. Bake for about 25 minutes until the filling is just set and golden. Remove from the oven and let it stand for a few minutes before serving.

Crab and Ham Crêpes

Serves 4

This dish costs the earth, and it tastes ravishing – the piquant contrast of cream, crabmeat and sherry with the delicate smoked ham is very striking. And it is all made in about 10 minutes! Warning – don't waste your time (or the crabmeat) on ordinary smoked ham!

**8 crêpes, 6 inches (15 cm) across
(recipes pages 14 and 15)**

**12 oz (350 g) crabmeat, frozen or tinned
1 oz (25 g) butter
1 heaped tablespoon chopped chives, or minced spring onions
5 tablespoons dry sherry   8 fl oz (225 ml) double cream
pinch of salt   pinch of cayenne
1 egg yolk, size 3, beaten
dash of Worcestershire sauce
8 very thin slices of Westphalian ham,
prosciutto or Kassler Rippchen**

Preheat oven to 400°F/200°C/Gas 6.
1. Drain and dry the crabmeat, and sauté it in hot butter. Stir in the chives or spring onions, the sherry, cream, seasoning, egg yolk and Worcestershire sauce and cook on very low heat for 2 minutes.
2. Butter 4 shallow 6–7 inch (15–18 cm) ovenproof dishes and lay a crêpe in each. Put the ham slices on top in an even layer and spread with some of the creamed crab. Add another crêpe and finish with creamed crab. Bake for about 5 minutes near the top of the oven, and rush to the table.

Deep Fried
Cheese Crêpes

Makes 18, to serve with drinks

These are perfect to hand round with drinks. Try filling them with chopped ham and grated Cheddar, mixed with a little Meaux or Dijon mustard, salt and pepper and a little finely minced onion.

18 crêpes, 5 inches (13 cm) across
(recipes pages 14 and 15, reserving a little batter)

6 oz (175 g) mild Cheddar cheese, grated
2 spring onions or 2 shallots, finely chopped
salt
freshly ground black pepper
oil for deep frying

Preheat the oven to 350°F/180°C/Gas 4.
1. Mix together the grated cheese and the spring onions or shallots, and put a teaspoonful in the centre of each crêpe. Turn the top and bottom in, then fold in the sides and seal with a dab of left-over batter.
2. Heat the oil in a deep-fryer to 360°F/185°C and fry in batches, sealed-side down, until just brown. Drain well. Keep hot on kitchen paper on a baking sheet in the oven and serve as quickly as possible.

Arcadia Crêpes

Serves 6

There seems no reason why these crêpes should not be made with left-over brandy or rum butter if you have any to hand, but the kirsch-flavoured butter cream is more delicate and delicious. Be sparing with the jam, as too much sweetness here is cloying. This is a very quick and easy sweet.

12 crêpes, 6–7 inches (15–18 cm) across
(recipe page 14)

4 oz (100 g) icing sugar
2 oz (50 g) softened butter or margarine
2 tablespoons kirsch
12 scant teaspoons apricot or morello cherry jam
2 fl oz (50 ml) kirsch (optional)

1. In a medium-sized bowl, slowly cream together the sugar and the butter until smooth, and gradually stir in the kirsch. Spread the speckly side of each pancake with the butter, reserving about 2 tablespoons.
2. Put a scant teaspoon of whatever jam you like in the centre of each crêpe, fold the bottom and top over, then fold in the sides to make a neat parcel. Put the crêpes in a shallow ovenproof dish and spread the remaining kirsch butter over the top. The crêpes may now be refrigerated, covered with plastic film, until you are ready to bake them.
3. Preheat the oven to 350°F/180°C/Gas 4. Bake for about 15 minutes until the crêpes are heated through. Let them stand for a few minutes to cool slightly, then serve as they are or flamed with warmed kirsch.

Classic Blintzes

Serves 4–6

This famous Jewish-American dish is most often served as a sweet, usually with soured cream and sometimes with caster sugar scattered over the top.

12 crêpes, 6 inches (15 cm) across
(recipe page 14)

1–2 eggs, size 3
2 teaspoons caster sugar
good pinch of salt
12 oz (350 g) cream or curd cheese
2 oz (50 g) melted butter or margarine with a little oil
soured cream

1. Beat the eggs with the sugar and salt, then mix into the cheese. Lay out the crêpes, brown side uppermost. Put 1 tablespoon of the cheese mixture in the centre of each, fold the sides in, then turn the bottom and top in to make a neat parcel. If necessary, seal the joins with cold water. The blintzes may now be refrigerated until frying time.
2. In a wide heavy frying pan, heat the butter with the oil until it is hot but not browned. Put the blintzes in seam-side up, and fry until the bottom is golden-brown, turn and cook the second side for a slightly shorter time. Serve as quickly as you can – or keep them hot on folded kitchen paper in a warm oven (about 300°F/150°C/Gas 2) for up to 15 minutes. Hand round a bowl of very cold soured cream.

Jaffa Pancakes

Serves 4

Try using Margaret Smythe's Orange Liqueur (page 92) in this recipe. It is a wonderful standby at considerably less cost than the famous ones – indispensable if you are seriously into making crêpes.

12–16 orange pancakes, 6–7 inches (15–18 cm) across (recipe page 20)

3 fl oz (75 ml) whipping cream
½ teaspoon grated orange rind
1 teaspoon orange liqueur
caster sugar (optional)

1. Keep the pancakes hot while you make the sauce (see Master Directions, pages 12–13). Whip the cream to stiff peaks and very gently mix in the grated orange rind and liqueur. Taste, and add a little caster sugar if you like.
2. Spread each pancake with the sauce and serve flat on hot plates.

Black Forest Crêpes

Serves 6

Chocolate and cherries seem to have a mysterious affinity. The ingredients for this extremely simple, but very spectacular, recipe can be at hand well in advance: crème pâtissière with some almond flavouring added, crêpes cooked hours before, and reheated, and a very quick cherry sauce made from jam and water.

18 chocolate crêpes, 6 inches (15 cm) across
(recipe page 19)

6 oz (175 g) morello cherry jam
hot water
6 oz (175 g) crème pâtissière flavoured with 3 drops of almond essence
(see page 46)

1. Keep the crêpes hot while you prepare the sauce (see Master Directions, pages 12–13). Thin the cherry jam with about 2 tablespoons of hot water and gently heat, stirring.
2. Put 1 tablespoon of crème pâtissière in the centre of each crêpe, and roll up into a thin cigar shape. Put three crêpes on each warmed dessert plate, spread the crêpes with the hot cherry sauce and serve at once.

Simple Crêpes Suzette

Serves 6

This is the quick, easy and not very expensive version of what is to my mind a greatly overrated crêpe dish. For the classic, and more costly version, see opposite.

12 crêpes, 6–7 inches (15–18 cm) across
(recipe page 14)

3 oz (75 g) butter
3 oz (75 ml) orange liqueur (see page 92)
3 oz (75 ml) orange juice
4 tablespoons caster sugar
3 tablespoons brandy

1. Heat the butter, orange liqueur, orange juice and caster sugar in a small saucepan until bubbling.
2. Pour the sauce into a shallow frying pan and, one at a time, slide the crêpes in. Turn each crêpe over in the sauce, and with a large spoon and fork fold in half and then in half again. Push the folded crêpes against the sides of the frying pan. The sauce will begin to thicken slightly.
3. Pour the brandy into a cup and tip it into the centre of the frying pan. Let it warm through, then carefully set it alight. With a long spoon, baste the crêpes until the flame dies down. Serve at once on heated plates.

Classic Crêpes Suzettes

Serves 6

If you can do Step 3 in a chafing dish at the table, it is very spectacular.

**12 crêpes, 6–7 inches (15–18 cm) across
(recipe page 14)**

GRAND MARNIER BUTTER
**2 large, bright-skinned oranges
4 large sugar cubes, or 8 small ones
1½ oz (40 g) caster sugar
6 oz (175 g) unsalted butter
2 fl oz (50 ml) Grand Marnier (or any orange liqueur)**

TO FINISH
**2 tablespoons caster sugar
2 fl oz (50 ml) *each* brandy and Grand Marnier**

1. Rub the skins of the oranges with sugar lumps until soaked with fragrant oil. Peel the oranges very thinly. Mince the peel finely with caster sugar, then crush in the sugar cubes. Squeeze out orange juice.
2. Beat the butter and sugar until creamy, trickle in 3 fl oz (75 ml) strained orange juice, beating well, and finally beat in the Grand Marnier. Refrigerate.
3. In a frying pan, gently heat the butter to bubbling. Add the crêpes, turn, fold into quarters and push to sides of pan. Warm the sugar and alcohol in the centre of the pan, then ignite carefully. With a long spoon, slide the crêpes into the flaming sauce and baste cautiously. Serve when flame dies.

Coffee Chestnut Crêpes

Serves 6

This sinfully rich pudding is incredibly simple – but your lucky recipients must be sitting waiting as it will not stand. Despite its millionaire flavour, it is not very expensive to prepare. (Do not make the mistake of using tinned chestnut *purée* – it won't do.)

**12 freshly-made hot crêpes, 7–8 inches (18–20 cm) across
(recipe page 14)**

**2 teaspoons powdered coffee
scant 2 tablespoons boiling water
8 oz (225 g) tinned chestnut spread
2 tablespoons dark rum
8 fl oz (225 ml) whipping cream**

1. Mix the coffee powder with the boiling water, and stir into the chestnut spread. Blend with 1 tablespoon of the rum. Whip the cream with the remaining rum and gently fold half of it into the chestnut mixture. Chill.
2. Spread the hot crêpes with the cold chestnut cream, roll them and rush them to the table. Pass round the remaining rum-flavoured whipped cream separately.

Craig's Crêpes

Serves 6

I have to thank Craig Claiborne, of the *New York Times*, for generously allowing me to use this recipe. The sauce is made well in advance, and the crêpes can be made as much as 8 hours ahead, kept separate with pieces of greaseproof paper. Reheat, and the whole luxurious dish can be put together in about 8 minutes.

6 crêpes, 8–10 inches (20–25 cm) across
(recipe page 14, with 1 tablespoon grated lemon rind stirred
into the batter)

1½ oz (40 g) butter or very good margarine
3 oz (75 g) icing sugar
good pinch of salt
1 teaspoon kirsch (or more, to taste)
½ teaspoon grated lemon rind
2 fl oz (50 ml) single cream or top of milk

1. Cream the butter, then beat in the sugar and salt. Stir in the remaining ingredients and beat until fluffy and thick. Chill.
2. Heat the crêpes (see Master Directions, pages 12–13), put them on hot individual dessert plates, spread each with the chilled butter and serve at once.

Irish Coffee Crêpes

Serves 6

If you prefer, use Irish whiskey instead of Irish Mist, increasing the amount of sugar to about 3 oz (75 g). But do not use a creamy Irish liqueur as this upsets the balance of the sauce, which is already as rich as the unwary digestion can deal with. My Dublin friend says that this is a dish for Shrove Tuesday night, with forty days of abstinence from all earthly delights to follow.

12 crêpes, 6–8 inches (15–20 cm) across
(recipe page 14)

3 oz (75 g) plain dark dessert chocolate
3 fl oz (75 ml) Irish Mist liqueur
scant 2 oz (50 g) caster sugar
3 egg yolks, size 3, beaten
pinch of salt
5 fl oz (150 ml) double cream

1. Melt the chocolate with the liqueur in a small saucepan set over simmering water. Stir in the sugar and cook until it dissolves. Stir 1 heaped tablespoon of the mixture into the well-beaten egg yolks and salt, then beat this into the sauce off the heat.
2. Whip the cream to stiff peaks and gently fold into the chocolate mixture, which will be fairly stiff, so be patient. Chill.
3. Heat the crêpes (see Master Directions, pages 12–13), spread each with a layer of the Irish Coffee Cream and serve instantly.

Key Lime Tarts

Serves 6

This is an adaptation of a classic Florida recipe. Crêpe cups may be used instead of tart shells for any sweet or savoury mixture.

**6 freshly-made crêpes, 6 inches (15 cm) across
(recipe page 14)**

**6 oz (175 g) caster sugar
2 tablespoons cornflour
pinch of salt
6 fl oz (175 ml) cold water *or* 4 fl oz (100 ml) water mixed with
2 fl oz (50 ml) light rum
2 eggs, size 3, separated
3 tablespoons lime juice   grated rind of 1 lime
a few drops of green food colouring**

1. Well oil the outsides of deep patty tins or dariole moulds and press freshly-made crêpes – neatly trimmed to perfect rounds – firmly against them. Bake upside down in a preheated oven at 375°F/190°C/Gas 5 for about 15 minutes until crisp. Cool on the tins before removing.
2. Mix the sugar, cornflour and salt in a heavy saucepan and gradually stir in the water. Whisk the egg yolks with the lime juice and rind, and add to the pan. Cook, stirring, on a low heat until thick and smooth. Add the food colouring and cool.
3. Whisk the egg whites to stiff peaks, scrape the lime custard on top, and gently cut the mixtures together. Spoon into the crêpe cups just before serving. Top with whipped cream if desired.

Lemon Crêpe Cake

Serves 4

Big crêpes look daunting, but are surprisingly easy to make: loosen completely with a long flexible palette knife, pull up the edge with your fingers and turn quickly. The simple lemon sauce is equally good with Wholewheat Crêpes (page 15).

5 crêpes, 10 inches (25 cm) across
(recipes pages 14 and 16)

3 oz (75 g) caster sugar
generous 1 tablespoon cornflour
8 fl oz (225 ml) water
very generous 1 oz (about 35–40 g) butter or margarine
½ teaspoon grated lemon rind
generous 1½ tablespoons lemon juice
pinch of salt
icing sugar

1. Keep the crêpes hot (see Master Directions, pages 12–13).
2. Mix the sugar, cornflour and water in the top of a double boiler and cook over gently boiling water until thick and smooth. Stir in the butter, lemon rind, lemon juice and salt, and cook for a further few minutes, stirring. (This stage can be prepared in advance, the sauce cooled and reheated over hot water.)
3. Spread four of the crêpes with the hot sauce, then stack them and put the remaining plain crêpe on top. Dust with icing sugar. Serve on a heated plate, and cut into four.

Copenhagen Crêpes

Serves 6

A very easy-to-make recipe (taking about 10 minutes from beginning to end). The crêpes can be made in advance and frozen; when thawed, they are simply stacked and not rolled.

12 crêpes, 6–7 inches (15–18 cm) across
(recipes pages 14, 15 and 16)

5 fl oz (125 ml) double cream
4 oz (100 g) lightly toasted flaked almonds, chopped
3 tablespoons icing sugar
a few drops of almond essence

Preheat the oven to 400°F/200°C/Gas 6.
1. Whip the cream so that it forms soft peaks. Stir in the chopped almonds, 2 tablespoons of the icing sugar and the almond essence. Spread about 1 tablespoon on each crêpe and stack them in a buttered shallow oven dish. Spread the remaining cream over the top crêpe.
2. Bake for about 5 minutes. Dust with the remaining icing sugar and cut in wedges to serve.

Crêpes Chambord

Serves 6

This recipe is a very much simplified version of one that originated in the Loire Valley. The filling is a sort of orange crème pâtissière.

12 crêpes, 6–7 inches (15–18 cm) across
(recipe page 14)

2 heaped tablespoons white flour
2 level tablespoons cornflour
pinch of salt
3 egg yolks, size 2 or 3
15 fl oz (425 ml) milk
grated rind of 1 large, bright-skinned orange and half a lemon
2 tablespoons double cream
4 tablespoons orange liqueur (see page 92)
1–2 tablespoons icing sugar

1. Sift the flour with the cornflour and salt into a heavy saucepan. Whisk the egg yolks with the milk, rind and sugar, and gradually stir into the cornflour. Bring slowly to the boil, stirring constantly, and reaching all round the bottom of the pan with a wooden spoon. Turn the heat to very low and continue cooking until the mixture is thick and velvety. Cool to lukewarm and stir in the cream and liqueur.
2. Preheat the grill. Put 1 heaped tablespoon of filling down the centre of each crêpe, roll and lay seam-side down in a shallow buttered heat-proof dish. Cover well with sifted icing sugar and grill, watching with an eagle eye, until darkly caramelised.

Oranjeboom Crêpes

Serves 6

Chocolate and orange go wonderfully well together, as this Dutch recipe shows. Oranjeboom Crêpes can be made up to 8 hours in advance.

**12 crêpes, 7–8 inches (18–20 cm) across
(recipes pages 14 and 15)**

**6 oz (175 g) caster or granulated sugar
1½ oz (40 g) cornflour
pinch of salt
9 fl oz (250 ml) orange juice
grated rind of half a large orange
2 oz (50 g) butter or margarine
2 oz (50 g) plain dark dessert chocolate
6 oz (175 g) icing sugar
½ teaspoon vanilla essence
3 tablespoons boiling water**

1. Mix together the sugar, cornflour and salt. Stir in the orange juice and cook on low heat, stirring, until thick and smooth. Add the rind and 1 oz (25 g) butter. Stir well, then leave to cool, covered. Do not stir.
2. Spread about 2 tablespoons of the filling on the speckled side of each crêpe, leaving a margin of about ½ inch (1.5 cm) around the edge. Roll up and place, seam-side down, on greaseproof paper.
3. Melt the chocolate over very low heat with the remaining butter. Stir in the icing sugar and vanilla, and gradually blend in the boiling water to make a thin syrup. Pour 1 tablespoonful over each crêpe, and chill.

The Flames of Rome

Serves 4

This quite spectacular recipe came from a restaurant in Italy – and it is rich, luscious and rather costly, as you can see. Serve it after a very plain main course!

**8 crêpes, 6–7 inches (15–18 cm) across
(recipe page 14)**

**generous 1 oz (25–30 g) *each* of walnuts, hazelnuts and almonds, all
finely chopped
2 generous tablespoons clear honey
2 tablespoons butter or good margarine
2 tablespoons caster sugar
5 fl oz (150 ml) orange juice
2 tablespoons *each* of brandy, rum and orange liqueur**

1. Mix the chopped nuts with the honey and 1 tablespoon of the butter. Spread one half of each crêpe with some of the mixture, fold down the other side and fold again into quarters.
2. Melt the remaining butter with the sugar and orange juice in a wide frying pan. Put in the crêpes and heat them through, turning once.
3. Meanwhile, heat the alcohol in a small saucepan placed in a larger pan of hot water (*not* on direct heat). Take the crêpe pan off the heat, pour on the heated liqueurs and set alight. Baste with a long-handled spoon. When the flame dies, serve at once on heated plates.

Quebec Crêpes

Serves 6

A spectacular dish. Once filled, the crêpes can stand for 2–3 hours before baking but cook them a little longer before flaming with orange liqueur.

**12 crêpes, 6–7 inches (15–18 cm) across
(recipe page 14)**

**3 tablespoons cornflour   2 rounded tablespoons caster sugar
8 fl oz (225 ml) single cream
2 eggs, size 3, separated   ½ teaspoon vanilla essence
2 tablespoons butter
pinch of cream of tartar   2 tablespoons caster sugar
2 teaspoons lemon juice
6 tablespoons orange liqueur (see page 92)**

1. In a saucepan, stir together the cornflour and sugar, then gradually blend in the cream. Stirring constantly, slowly bring to the boil and cook until thick and smooth. Cool slightly, then stir in beaten egg yolks and cook, stirring, on a *very* low heat until the mixture thickens. Add the vanilla, cover tightly and chill for up to 24 hours.
2. Preheat the oven to 400°F/200°C/Gas 6. Dot a shallow casserole with the butter. Beat the egg whites with the cream of tartar until foamy, then gradually beat in the sugar until stiff. Stir 1 tablespoon of meringue into the chilled cream, then gently fold the two mixtures together. Fill each crêpe, fold in edges and put seam-side down in the casserole.
3. Bake for 10 minutes until risen, then add the lemon juice. Warm the liqueur in a saucepan, set it alight and pour it over the crêpes.

Crepricots

Serves 6

This recipe is much nicer made with rather thick crêpes, not the tissue-thin ones. And it is so quick to do, as both crêpes and sauce can be made well in advance. Do not over-sweeten the apricots.

12 crêpes, 6–7 inches (15–18 cm) across
(recipes pages 14 and 15, but made with 3 oz [75 g] flour to 8 fl oz
[225 ml] liquid)

6 oz (175 g) dried apricots
15 fl oz (425 ml) water
2 oz (50 g) soft light brown sugar
1 teaspoon vanilla essence
3 oz (75 g) flaked almonds, toasted

1. Simmer the apricots in water for about 25 minutes, or until soft but not mushy. Add the sugar and vanilla, and cook for another 5–10 minutes. Cool and crush apricots with a cooking spoon, but do not purée. Chill.
2. Heat the crêpes (see Master Directions, pages 12–13). Serve two crêpes per person. Spread each with the cold apricot sauce, scatter on the almonds and hurry to the table.

Czardas Pancakes

Serves 6

Frighteningly rich! Despite its Hungarian name the recipe comes from a pre-Revolution Russian source. Only serve after a plain meal.

12 crêpes, 6 inches (15 cm) across (recipe page 14)

3 oz (75 g) plain dark chocolate, grated
3 oz (75 g) hazelnuts or walnuts, finely chopped
4 oz (100 g) caster sugar   2 oz (50g) sultanas
1 heaped tablespoon grated orange rind
1 oz (25 g) chilled butter

SAUCE
5 fl oz (150 ml) whipping cream
1 teaspoon rum or ½ teaspoon vanilla essence
2 egg yolks, size 3   1 oz (25 g) icing sugar

Preheat the oven to 350°F/180°C/Gas 4.
1. Mix the chocolate with the nuts, sugar, sultanas and orange rind. Spread this mixture evenly over each crêpe, and stack them in a buttered baking dish, finishing with a plain (unspread) crêpe. Shave the chilled butter in flakes over the top.
2. Whip the cream with the rum or vanilla to soft peaks. Whisk together the egg yolks and icing sugar until thick and pale, and lightly fold into the whipped cream. Set aside.
3. Bake the crêpes for about 10 minutes until heated through. Cut in wedges. Serve with the whipped cream sauce.

PANCAKES

drop scones • wheatcakes • stack of wheats • griddle cakes • hot cakes • flannel cakes • flapjacks • Scotch pancakes

Pancakes, which appear in North American cookery under all the names listed above, are much heartier and more robust than the thin European crêpe. Their ancestry is German, Scandinavian or Scottish – this quick and satisfying form of bread usually appears in countries where the winters are long and severe and where, in the past, supplies of food have had to be hoarded and eked out.

English visitors to the United States who encounter 'flapjacks' or 'hotcakes' for breakfast either love them or hate them. Those reared on the great traditional English breakfast – with eggs, bacon, fried bread, grilled tomatoes, and strong tea – often quail before a stack of hot hearty pancakes dripping with butter and accompanied by a jar of maple syrup. In fact, these north American pancakes are very similar to the Scottish or English drop scone: served hot off the girdle (griddle), dripping with butter, and offered with honey or jam. Drop scones are quick to bake, universally loved, and make a winter tea-time far more special than do commercially produced breads and biscuits.

The famous American breakfast of pancakes, crisp bacon or pure pork sausages and maple syrup is served coast to coast, winter and summer. But pancakes are equally well-known as a substantial lunch or supper dish, with any savoury topping you choose to make – chicken à la king, creamed ham with mushrooms, curried eggs, fish or meat in a rich sauce. Savoury pancakes are a wonderful way of making something out of almost nothing; perhaps that is why so many such recipes are found in the hand-written 'receipt books' of New England and Canadian women who lived by the rule, 'use it up, make it last, make it do'.

Pancakes are very quick to make. The batter needs no resting time and can be mixed in about two minutes. You can make your own pancake mix, too (see formula, page 56).

Pans and girdles (griddles)

No special equipment is needed for making pancakes – merely a heavy, wide frying pan or a girdle (griddle), and a palette knife or slice. Non-stick pans are useful, but to make the perfect pancake they must be handled with care and not heated too fast on a high heat or scratched with palette knives or cleaning materials.

Heavy cast-iron girdles look wonderful in photographs of interiors of Scottish cottages, and they do make superb pancakes once they are seasoned and aged (for which read an ever-deepening layer of invisible grease and not too much washing). But they are devils to clean, and they rust.

Never plunge a frying pan or girdle into cold water when it is hot because this causes even a heavy one to warp, and your pancakes will not be perfect rounds but wild trapezoids and triangles. They will taste the same, but as part of their attraction is the pretty, even-sized rounds, the shape does matter.

Master Directions

1. Never over-beat batter: mix the dry and liquid ingredients with strong strokes of a large spoon, or with a hand-whisk or on the lowest speed of an electric mixer. Over-beating makes pancakes tough. Pancake batter is fairly thick and should drip lazily from a spoon or jug. It is more like English drop scone batter than the thin 'pouring' crêpe batter.

2. Heat your frying pan or girdle (griddle) on moderate heat until drops of cold water dance and skitter like mercury. If the water disappears at once, the pan is too hot; if it merely steams, it is too cool.

3. Put a little oil in a saucer, lightly dip a folded pad of kitchen paper into it, and wipe the paper across the pan's surface. Do not leave the pad soaking in the oil, rest it on the side of the saucer. You may or may not have to grease the pan between batches. The surface should look satiny, not greasy.

4. Pour the batter in well-spaced pools from a lipped jug or bowl: the best pancakes are about 5 inches (13 cm) across and just under ¼ inch (5 mm) thick, but it does depend on the recipe.

5. Cook for 1 or 2 minutes, until the upper surface of the pancake looks bubbly and slightly dry. Lift the edge with a palette knife or slice, and if the bottom is smooth and golden, flip the pancake. Cook for about half the time on the second side.

6. Keep the pancakes warm on a wide plate set over a saucepan of simmering water. If they must stand for more than a few minutes, separate the pancakes in the folds of a clean warm tea-towel, or with greaseproof paper strips. Ideally, pancakes should be lifted straight off the pan on to waiting plates, but that means that the cook must be prepared to be the last to eat!

Note: You can make the batter in advance and let it stand overnight, refrigerated and covered. *Never* leave yeast-raised pancake batters, or those containing whisked egg whites, to stand once they are ready to bake.

Resting the batter: I have never found that it makes the slightest difference to 'rest' the batter, but do it if it suits you. These hearty pancakes were often made for breakfast by campfire cooks for hungry lumberjacks or cowhands, and the cook would have been lynched if the meal was late.

Universal Pancake Mix

Makes 2 lb (1 kg) of dry mix

This incredibly useful pancake mix makes perfect American-type break-fast pancakes: substantial and satisfying, with glossy brown surfaces and pale cream edges. They are tender, soft and irresistible.

1½ lb (750 g) flour: plain white, 85% light brown, or wholewheat
1 tablespoon salt
3 teaspoons baking powder
3 oz (75 g) powdered milk
8 oz (225 g) white cooking fat

Sift the flour with the salt, baking powder and powdered milk, twice. Cut in the fat with a knife and rub in with the fingers until the mixture feels like fine breadcrumbs. Store in an absolutely dry, airtight tin or jar. This mix will keep for at least six months in a cool place.

TO MAKE 12–14 PANCAKES, 5 INCHES (13 CM) ACROSS

2 eggs, size 3 or 4
8 oz (225 g) dry mix
about 8 fl oz (225 ml) liquid: half milk, half water

1. Whisk the eggs and stir them into the dry mix, then gradually add the liquid (you may need a little more, depending on the type of flour in the mix). Stir well but do not over-beat. You are aiming for the consistency of a thick pouring custard, not a thin crêpe batter.
2. Cook according to Master Directions, pages 54–55.

American Classic Pancakes

Makes 16 pancakes, 4–5 inches (10–13 cm) across

This is the Sunday Morning Special – served with bacon, small sausages, maple syrup or honey, whipped butter or honey butter (see pages 92–93), and all the Sunday newspapers. These pancakes are thickish, light and tender. Leave out the sugar, and the same formula makes a wonderful base for any savoury creamed mixture.

8 oz (225 g) flour (see page 8)
1 tablespoon caster sugar
4 teaspoons baking powder
1 teaspoon salt
2 eggs, size 3 or 4
12 fl oz (350 ml) milk
2 oz (50 g) margarine or butter, melted

1. Sift the dry ingredients together into a bowl. Whisk the eggs, milk and melted butter together, and lightly stir into the dry ingredients until all the flour is moistened, but do not over-beat.
2. Cook according to Master Directions, pages 54–55. This batter thickens as it stands, so you will need to give it a good stir between cooking each batch of pancakes.

Maine Loggers' Flapjacks

Makes about 8 thick pancakes, 8–10 inches (20-25 cm) across

'Flapjack' is one of the many American names for breakfast pancakes – others are hot cakes, griddle cakes, wheatcakes, flannel cakes. This is a stick-to-the-ribs, *big* pancake, meant to see a woodsman through a cold Maine day. Serve it with 'country sausages' – spicy, herby and thick.

7 oz (200 g) strong white flour
½ teaspoon salt
1 teaspoon baking powder
1 teaspoon bicarbonate of soda
4 fl oz (100 ml) buttermilk, or soured milk (to sour milk, stir 1 generous teaspoon of lemon juice into the milk and let it stand for 5 minutes)
8 fl oz (225 ml) milk
1 egg, size 3
bacon dripping to grease the pan or girdle

1. Sift the flour, salt and baking powder into a large bowl. Stir the bicarbonate into the buttermilk or soured milk, add the fresh milk and the egg and beat the mixture well. Stir (do not beat) the liquid into the dry ingredients.
2. Bake according to the Master Directions, pages 54–55. The top of the flapjacks should look dull, and when the bubbles begin to break, this is the time to flip them over. This batter is thick and it separates quickly, so give it a good stir between batches.

Cornmeal Cakes

Makes about 20 pancakes, 5 inches (13 cm) across

Not to be confused with corn fritters, these slightly crunchy corn pancakes are marvellously tasty served with any savoury mixture, as well as for breakfast. They can be used as 'Tacos' (page 72) or with a curry instead of chapattis.

7 oz (200 g) coarse or medium cornmeal (not fine)
3 oz (75 g) white or wholemeal flour
½ teaspoon salt
½ teaspoon bicarbonate of soda
2 eggs, size 3 or 4
15 fl oz (425 ml) buttermilk or soured milk (to sour milk, stir 4
tablespoons lemon juice into milk and let it stand for 5 minutes)

1. Mix the cornmeal, flour, salt and bicarbonate very well. Whisk the eggs into the buttermilk and gradually stir into the dry ingredients. The mixture will be fairly thick, like a dropping cake batter.
2. Bake as in the Master Directions, pages 54–55. Stir the batter well between each batch as it settles very quickly.

Oven Pancakes

Serves 4

A super-special Sunday breakfast dish, made very quickly and topped with soft fruit, honey or syrup. Alternatively, serve it as a simple family pudding. It can be made in four individual ovenproof shallow dishes, with the butter heated in the oven before the batter is added. Very different from any other pancake.

1 oz (25 g) wholewheat or 85% flour
1 oz (25 g) white flour
4 fl oz (100 ml) milk, at room temperature
2 eggs, size 3
pinch of salt
1 oz (25 g) margarine or butter
½ teaspoon vegetable oil

Preheat the oven to 425°F/220°C/Gas 7.
1. Beat the flours, milk and eggs together until thoroughly blended, but do not over-beat. Add the salt. Melt the butter with the oil in a 9 inch (23 cm) ovenproof frying pan or a flameproof shallow casserole. When it sizzles, pour in the batter and put in the oven.
2. Bake for about 15 minutes, until the pancake is risen and golden. Serve with any soft fruit, slightly crushed, or honey or golden syrup.

Rice Pancakes

Makes about 16 pancakes, 4 inches (10 cm) across

Serve the sweet version for breakfast or tea with honey or golden syrup, or with cold butter alone. Savoury rice pancakes go beautifully with curries or goulashes, instead of the usual plain rice.

SWEET
generous 6 oz (175 g) cooked long-grain rice
8 fl oz (225 ml) milk
1 tablespoon vegetable oil
4 oz (100 g) flour
generous 2 teaspoons caster sugar
good pinch of mixed spice
pinch of salt
2 teaspoons baking powder
butter or margarine, to fry

1. Mix all the main ingredients together. Heat about 1 teaspoon of butter or margarine in a heavy frying pan or girdle. Drop the batter by tablespoonfuls, spreading it slightly, and cook until the undersides are brown. Turn once.

SAVOURY
Use the same recipe as above, but omit the sugar and add 1 teaspoon of finely chopped chives, spring onions, or mixed herbs.

Sourdough (Alaska) Pancakes

Makes about 40 pancakes, 5 inches (13 cm) across

This is a simplified version of the classic American sourdough pancake, which involves about eight steps and can take over your life! These pancakes are thick, hearty and with an agreeable, slightly sour, tang. Stir the batter between batches as it settles quickly. Bacon, sausages, maple syrup or honey are the traditional accompaniments.

15 fl oz (425 ml) warm water
2 teaspoons dry yeast
12 oz (350 g) white or 85% flour
1 teaspoon salt
½ teaspoon bicarbonate of soda
1½ tablespoons black treacle, mixed with 1½ tablespoons golden syrup
4 fl oz (100 ml) warm water
2 eggs, size 2

1. Whisk the 15 fl oz (425 ml) warm water and the dry yeast together. Leave it to stand for a few minutes in a warm place until it has a good frothy head, then stir in the flour. Cover the bowl and let it stand for 24 hours at room temperature.
2. Add the salt, bicarbonate, treacle mixture, and an additional 4 fl oz (100 ml) warm water. Beat the eggs well and stir into the batter until just mixed, do not beat! Let the batter stand for 30 minutes and bake according to the Master Directions, pages 54–55.

Blini

Makes about 24 pancakes, 2–3 inches (5–7½ cm) across, to serve 6 as a starter

This is a quick, twentieth-century version of the traditional Russian delicacy, which was always made with yeast 24 hours in advance of serving. Buckwheat grows in immense swathes, miles across, in Russia and is the basis of many of their staple dishes. Buckwheat flour can usually be found in health food shops.

5 oz (150 g) buckwheat flour
1 teaspoon baking powder
pinch of salt
½ teaspoon caster sugar
1 egg, size 3
5 fl oz (150 ml) soured cream
6 fl oz (175 ml) milk

1. Sift the dry ingredients together. Beat the egg with 2 tablespoons of the soured cream and all the milk. Stir into the dry mixture, mixing well but do not over-beat.
2. Bake as in the Master Directions, pages 54–55, dropping the batter by tablespoonfuls to make small pancakes.
3. Keep the blini warm on a plate over a saucepan of simmering water until all are cooked. Serve with the remaining soured cream, melted butter, black or red lumpfish 'caviar', or smoked salmon slices or trimmings.

Cheese Pancakes

Makes about 12 pancakes, 6–7 inches (15–18 cm) across

These pancakes are too thick to roll, and should be served folded in the centre over a savoury filling, with perhaps one of the following: chicken à la king (page 70), creamed curried eggs or fish, sautéed chicken livers with mushrooms, or as Shona's Pancakes (page 69).

8 oz (225 g) plain flour
8 fl oz (225 ml) milk
8 fl oz (225 ml) water
3 eggs, size 3
1 teaspoon salt
4–5 oz (100–150 g) Emmenthal or Cheddar cheese, grated

1. Sift the flour into a bowl and make a well in the centre. Whisk the milk, water, eggs and salt together and gradually stir into the flour. Mix well, but do not over-beat. Cover and let the batter rest for about 30 minutes.
2. Mix in the grated cheese. If the batter has thickened, thin it with about 2 tablespoons of water and stir well. Cook in a 6–7 inch (15–18 cm) omelette or crêpe pan.

Puffcakes

Makes about 24 pancakes, 3–4 inches (7½–10 cm) across, to serve 6

This makes a blissful simple pudding served with orange marmalade thinned with orange juice, and, if possible, a teaspoon of orange liqueur (see page 92 for Homemade Orange Liqueur). Or have them for breakfast with syrup or fruit.

6 eggs, size 3 or 4, separated
½ oz (12 g) butter or margarine, melted
2 oz (50 g) white or 85% flour
4 fl oz (100 ml) soured cream or yoghurt

1. Whisk the egg yolks until they are thick and lemon-coloured. Stir in the melted butter, flour and soured cream in alternate spoonfuls, stirring the mixture until it is just smooth. Do not over-beat.

2. Whisk the egg whites in a large bowl until stiff. Scoop 2 tablespoonfuls of the whisked egg whites into the batter and stir well, then pour the batter on top of the egg whites and lightly cut together.

3. Cook according to the Master Directions, pages 54–55. Drop the foamy batter by heaped tablespoonfuls, and cook until the top looks bubbly and slightly dry before turning over. This batter must be used up all in one go, it will not stand. Serve as a pudding, or for breakfast with syrup or soft fruit.

Scotch Pancakes or Drop Scones

Makes about 15–18 pancakes, 3 inches (7½ cm) across

These sweet tea pancakes are best served with cold butter only, I think, but you may want to have jam or honey as well. Two ounces (50 g) of sultanas may be added to the batter. Self-raising flour may be used, but the pancakes will not be quite as light.

1 oz (25 g) caster sugar
1 oz (25 g) butter or margarine, at room temperature
8 oz (225 g) plain flour
1 teaspoon bicarbonate of soda
2 teaspoons cream of tartar
1 egg, size 3 or 4, beaten
about 10 fl oz (275 ml) milk

1. Cream the sugar and the butter together. Sift the dry ingredients together, and add to the creamed mixture 2 tablespoons at a time, alternating with the beaten egg and milk. Stir well to form a thickish batter which will drop lazily from a lifted tablespoon.
2. Heat a heavy frying pan or girdle on a moderate heat, grease it lightly, and drop the batter a tablespoonful at a time. Cook on one side until the top begins to look bubbly and slightly dry, turn and cook the other side. Keep the pancakes warm in a concertina-folded tea-towel and serve as soon as possible.

Oatmeal Pancakes

Makes 16 pancakes, 3 inches (7½ cm) across

These are tea pancakes, very soft and slightly sweet, to be served with ice-cold butter – no jam or preserves.

2 oz (50 g) plus a tablespoon flour
½ teaspoon baking powder
2 oz (50 g) caster sugar
2 tablespoons fine cornmeal (optional)
8 fl oz (225 ml) buttermilk or soured milk (to sour milk, stir 1
tablespoon lemon juice into the milk and let it stand for 5 minutes)
1 teaspoon bicarbonate of soda
¼ teaspoon salt
4 tablespoons soured cream or yoghurt
1 egg, size 3
1 oz (25 g) porridge oats
cold butter

1. Sift together the flour, baking powder, sugar and cornmeal, if using. Mix together the buttermilk, bicarbonate of soda, salt and soured cream, and stir until foamy. Beat in the egg, and stir the liquid into the porridge oats. Add the dry ingredients to this mixture and stir thoroughly.
2. Cook as in Master Directions, pages 54–55, dropping the batter a heaped tablespoon at a time and spreading it slightly with the spoon. Cook on a medium heat as these pancakes are rather thick. Stir the batter between each batch.
3. Spread with butter, fold over and eat from the hand.

Sunset Sandwich

Serves 4

This is not a dainty crêpe dish but a substantial and satisfying snack or lunch. Cornmeal Cakes (page 59) form a superb base for a Sunset Sandwich.

8 hearty pancakes, 5 inches (13 cm) across
(recipes pages 57, 58 and 59)

2 oz (50 g) soft butter or margarine
16 very thin slices of mild onion
1 ripe avocado, sliced in 24 small slivers
2 tomatoes, peeled, each cut in 4 slices
8 rashers crisply-fried streaky bacon
8 thin slices of sharp Chedder cheese

Preheat the oven to 350°F/180°C/Gas 4.
1. Butter each pancake lightly. On each one, make layers of 2 slices of onion, 3 slivers of avocado, a slice of tomato, a strip of bacon, a slice of cheese.
2. Bake on a lightly-buttered Swiss roll tin for about 10 minutes, until the cheese melts and bubbles. Serve at once.

Shona's Pancakes

Serves 6

This makes a delicious and quite filling vegetarian lunch or supper dish.

**12 freshly-made cheese pancakes, 6–7 inches (15–18 cm) across
(recipe page 64)**

SAUCE
**2 egg yolks, size 3
1 teaspoon lemon juice
3 fl oz (75 ml) hot water
4 oz (100 g) butter or margarine, melted
salt, pepper and a pinch of cayenne**

FILLING
**3 carrots, 2 large leeks, 4 stalks celery
3 oz (75 g) mushrooms, wiped
1 oz (25 g) butter or margarine**

1. In the top of an enamel-lined double boiler, over simmering water, mix the egg yolks, lemon juice and hot water and stir until smooth and slightly thickened. Slowly trickle in the hot butter and stir until the sauce thickens. Season and remove from the heat.
2. Cut the carrots, leeks and celery into small, thin strips. Slice the mushrooms. Melt the butter in a heavy frying pan and cook the vegetables slowly until soft but not coloured. Mix with the sauce and keep warm. Make the pancakes.
3. Pour the sauce on half of each pancake and fold the other half over.

Pancakes à la King

Serves 4 as a light luncheon dish

This is a wonderful way to use left-over chicken, stretching a few ounces into a meal.

**8–12 freshly made hearty pancakes, 4–5 inches (10–13 cm) across
(recipes pages 57 and 58)**

**4 oz (100 g) small white mushrooms, wiped and halved
generous 2 oz (50 g) butter or margarine
3 tablespoons plain flour
12 fl oz (350 ml) chicken stock or milk
1 egg yolk, size 2 or 3, beaten
8 oz (225 g) cooked chicken, boned and diced
2 oz (50 g) tinned sweet pimento, chopped
pinch of paprika
1–2 oz (25–50 g) flaked almonds (optional)
1 generous tablespoon dry sherry (optional)
salt and pepper**

1. In a saucepan, sauté the mushrooms in 1 oz (25 g) of the butter, and remove the mushrooms. Add the remaining butter, stir in the flour and cook for 2 minutes, stirring. Add the chicken stock or milk and bring slowly to the boil. Allow to cool slightly, then add the egg yolk.
2. Stir in the chicken, mushrooms, pimento, paprika, almonds and sherry and cook, stirring, over a very low heat until thick and heated through. Season. Allow 2–3 pancakes per person and pour the sauce over.

Pancake Pizza

Serves 4

A simply wonderful dish, and for those who don't like the traditional chewy bread-dough crust of pure pizza, this is a revelation. You can use any combination of toppings you like – sliced Italian salami or pepperoni, cooked tiny meatballs, tuna, tinned artichoke hearts or sautéed green peppers or red pimentos.

8 pancakes, 5 inches (13 cm) across
(recipes pages 57 and 58)

8 oz (225 g) bought or homemade tomato sauce
4–6 oz (100–175 g) Mozzarella or German Loaf cheese, sliced
3 oz (75 g) mushrooms, thinly sliced
1 oz (25 g) anchovy fillets
12 black olives
½ teaspoon dried basil
good pinch of dried oregano
2 oz (50 g) grated Parmesan cheese

Preheat the oven to 350°F/180°C/Gas 4.
1. Lightly grease a round, shallow ovenproof dish or tin, with a diameter 9–10 inches (23–25 cm). Lay in the pancakes, overlapping. Cover with sauce, cheese, mushrooms, anchovy fillets arranged in a lattice pattern, olives dotted evenly across the surface, and herbs. Scatter on the Parmesan.
2. Bake for about 25–30 minutes until the pizza is brown and bubbling.

Pancake Tacos

Serves 4 to 6

These pancake Tacos wouldn't fool a Mexican or a Texan, but they are a delicious, very sloppy hot-and-cold sandwich. Oddly enough, the recipe came from British Columbia! You can vary the fillings as you choose, with spicy relishes, avocado, shredded lettuce, etc.

12 cornmeal pancakes, 8 inches (20 cm) across
(recipe page 59)

3 oz (75 ml) soured cream or yoghurt
½ teaspoon dried red pepper flakes, or a good pinch of cayenne
6 oz (175 g) mild Cheddar cheese, grated
2 oz (50 g) onion, grated or finely chopped
2 medium ripe tomatoes, thinly sliced
salt   freshly ground black pepper

Preheat the oven to 350°F/180°C/Gas 4.
1. Lightly oil a Swiss roll tin. Fold each pancake in half and stuff it with a crumpled piece of aluminium foil so that it lies in a 'C' shape. Place the pancakes on the tin – if necessary, run a thin skewer through each so that they do not unroll. Bake for about 10 minutes near the top of the oven until crisp and fill immediately.
2. Meanwhile, mix the soured cream or yoghurt with the red pepper flakes or cayenne to taste.
3. Fill each hot 'taco' with some cheese, onion, and tomato. Sprinkle with salt and pepper and add a dollop of the soured cream mixture.

Sweetcorn Pancakes

Serves 6

This is a traditional American accompaniment to fried chicken, baked ham or fried rabbit, and equally delicious with bacon for breakfast. Not to be confused with corn fritters which are fried in deep fat.

2 eggs, size 3, separated
4 tablespoons white or 85% flour
½ teaspoon salt
freshly ground black pepper
14 oz (400 g) tin whole-kernel sweet corn
vegetable oil for frying

1. Whisk the egg yolks with the flour and seasonings, and stir in the corn. Whisk the egg whites to stiff peaks and scrape the corn batter in on top of them. Gently cut and fold together.
2. Heat a girdle (griddle) or heavy frying pan until drops of cold water dance on the surface. Add enough oil to make the pan very shiny (more oil than for ordinary pancakes). Drop the batter from a tablespoon and cook until the top is bubbly and the underside brown. Turn and cook the other side. The pancakes should be about 2 inches (5 cm) across.
3. Keep warm on kitchen paper on a plate set over simmering water until all the pancakes are cooked.

Potato Pancakes (Latkes)

Serves 4

A traditional Jewish-American dish, with, most probably, a German ancestry. Please don't write angry letters to me saying that this recipe doesn't match your mother-in-law's – because I know that already! There are 23 other versions in my file. This one is *my* mother-in-law's.

1½ lb (750 g) firm raw potatoes, peeled and grated
1 small onion, very finely chopped
4 fl oz (100 ml) milk
1 teaspoon salt
1 egg, size 2 or 3
2 tablespoons flour
butter or margarine mixed with a little oil, for frying

1. Mix the potato, onion and milk well. Add salt, egg and flour.
2. Heat the butter and oil in a heavy frying pan until it begins to sizzle but not brown. Drop in the potato mixture by heaped tablespoonfuls, spreading the pancakes slightly with the spoon. Cook for about 3 minutes on each side. Serve with pot roast, fried chicken or roast pork – and some cold, slightly sweetened apple purée.

Note: This mixture must be cooked as soon as it is made, as it turns a rather horrid and threatening grey colour if it is allowed to stand for even 10 minutes.

Courgette Pancakes

Serves 6

These pancakes make an interesting and different vegetable accompaniment. They taste very good indeed.

1½ lb (750 g) courgettes, topped and tailed
2 oz (50 g) flour
1 teaspoon baking powder
salt
freshly ground black pepper
1 egg, size 2 or 3
2 teaspoons olive or vegetable oil
2 oz (50 g) butter or margarine, melted
2 oz (50 g) grated Parmesan cheese

1. Chop the courgettes or shred them. Sift the flour, baking powder, salt and pepper together and stir into the courgettes. Beat the egg well and stir it in, then mix in the oil.
2. Grease well a heavy frying pan or girdle (griddle) and heat it until a drop of cold water dances on the surface. Drop in the courgette mixture by heaped tablespoonfuls and cook on medium heat for about 3 minutes, then turn and cook the other side. Keep warm on kitchen paper on a plate until all the pancakes are cooked. Serve with the melted butter poured on, and hand round the Parmesan separately.

Saucer Pancakes

Serves 4

These are more cake-like than the usual pancake or crêpe, and very sweet. They make a very simple, but quite delicious, pudding or tea-time treat. Shallow pie tins may be used instead of saucers.

2 oz (50 g) butter or margarine
2 oz (50 g) caster sugar
2 oz (50 g) flour
2 eggs, size 3, beaten
10 fl oz (275 ml) milk
butter
Filling: jam, lemon curd, or lemon juice and caster sugar

1. Cream the butter and sugar together. Stir in the flour, alternately with the beaten egg, a tablespoonful at a time. Blend in the milk gradually, and beat until smooth. Cover and leave to stand for 30 minutes.
2. Heat the oven to 350°F/180°C/Gas 4. Thickly butter four *old* saucers (6 inches/15 cm diameter) and divide the batter between them. Bake about 20 minutes, until brown and slightly risen.
3. Loosen with a palette knife and slide out on to individual plates. Spread with jam or lemon curd and fold over; or simply sprinkle the top with lemon juice and sugar. Serve hot.

Kaiserschmarren

Serves 6

The name means 'Emperor's Rags', and the story is that an eighteenth-century king took refuge in a peasant woman's house during a storm; she made him pancakes but in her nervousness tore them as they came from the hot pan. It became a traditional Austro-Hungarian dessert.

3 eggs, size 3
8 fl oz (225 ml) milk
4 oz (100 g) white flour
1 teaspoon caster sugar
pinch of salt
5 oz (150 g) butter or margarine, melted
2 oz (50 g) flaked almonds   2 oz (50 g) sultanas
icing sugar
cinnamon (optional)

1. Stir together the eggs, milk, flour, sugar and salt to make a smooth batter. Heat a heavy 9 inch (23 cm) frying pan and pour in about 2 tablespoonfuls of the melted butter. Add about 1 tablespoon each of almonds and sultanas to the pan and pour in about a half teacup of batter.
2. Brown on medium heat, turn and cook the other side. Slide out on to a hot dish and keep warm while you make the rest of the pancakes. Add about 1 tablespoon of melted butter and 1 tablespoon each of almonds and sultanas for each succeeding pancake.
3. With two forks, tear the pancakes into small irregular pieces, and dust with icing sugar and cinnamon.

WAFFLES

Hot waffles, which have been enormously popular for the greater part of the twentieth century in the United States and Canada, have recently seized the imagination of the British public, with the introduction of several types of electric wafflemakers. As these often have the added bonus of an interchangeable plate for making *croque monsieur* or other toasted sandwiches, they are very good value. It is a little too early to say whether or not waffles will become a part of the way of life in Britain as they are in America. From the 1900s onwards, when electric waffle-irons were first invented, American Sunday breakfast parties have often featured waffles with a variety of syrups, jams and fruit sauces set forth decoratively in crystal and silver dishes. I can remember my mother and her friends presiding over Sunday-evening waffle suppers, with creamed savoury mixtures simmering in a copper chafing dish over dancing flames.

Waffle batter, always made with melted butter or oil, is richer and more luxurious than pancake batter, and so waffles are as filling and satisfying to the palate as they are to the eyes. They are equally delicious served with crisp grilled sausages or bacon and golden syrup for a gala breakfast, or with a savoury topping such as creamed chicken and mushrooms.

In Belgium and France, waffle-sellers are a familiar sight, making and vending crisp light *gauffres* and *gauffrettes* from pavement stalls and serving them with a dusting of icing sugar or a scoop of ice-cream. Waffles and ice-cream seem to be born to be partners. Indeed, ice-cream cones (cornets) were invented at the St Louis (Missouri) World's Fair of 1904, when an ice-cream seller ran out of small serving dishes and was rescued by a quick-witted waffle-seller who twirled his thin round waffles into cones and saved the day.

Waffles freeze perfectly, and can be quickly heated up from their frozen state in an electric toaster or under a grill – which makes them ideal standbys for last-minute meals. While working on these recipes, I discovered that crisp waffles (chocolate or ginger, lemon or raisin) can double as wonderful sweet biscuits, while spicy cheese waffles cut in small squares are delicious served with drinks. Waffles always seem 'special' and as they are so easy to make in the versatile new machines, it is well worth giving them a try.

Waffle Irons

Electric waffle-makers are usually thermostatically controlled, and some have indicator lights which show when the correct temperature has been reached. Waffle batter contains a good deal of fat (melted butter or oil), and, once the iron is 'run in' according to the manufacturer's instructions, it is often not necessary to oil the waffle plates before use.

A few small non-electric waffle irons can be bought, and sometimes an old one with a highly decorative 'weave' or honeycomb pattern turns up in an antique shop. These are used on top of the cooker – according to the maker's directions, or until a few drops of cold water dance and bounce on the hot surface. Usually they need to be oiled before using, and again after being thoroughly washed and dried before storing. They are not very large and are most satisfactory for a one- or two-person family – unless you are prepared to spend a lot of time making and freezing waffles for future use.

To clean any type of waffle iron, allow it to cool and use a small stiff brush (an old toothbrush, perhaps) to whisk out the crumbs. Non-stick plates on electric waffle irons usually need no washing unless they have become very greasy with use.

Master Directions

1. Mix the batter quickly, by hand or on the slow speed of an electric mixer. Do not over-beat, as this makes for tough waffles.

2. Heating: follow carefully the directions for your own waffle iron. Most electric irons are thermostatically controlled and will indicate when the waffle is baked. Otherwise, wait until the iron has stopped steaming, and very gently test by pulling up the top of the iron. Never force it, as the waffle will tear beyond repair. Let it cook a minute or two longer.

3. Always put waffles on a wire rack, either to keep warm in a cool oven (225°F/110°C/Gas ¼) or to cool for later reheating. Stacking them on a plate will make them soggy.

4. Waffles, either frozen or fresh, reheat well in an electric toaster or under the grill. Watch them as they burn easily, especially the ones with sugar, treacle or fruit in the mixture. Under a grill, they need only be heated on one side.

5. Many waffle batters can be made in advance. Keep the batter in a covered jug and refrigerate for several hours or overnight. Stir well before using. Those batters made with whisked egg whites or yeast, however, must be used as soon as they are made.

6. Freezing: see page 9.

Note: all the waffles in this book were made on a Tefal French electric iron, and quantities refer to its capacity. Other irons may make larger or smaller waffles.

American Waffles

Makes 6

These crisp light waffles are traditionally served for breakfast with grilled bacon, ham, sausages and melted butter, plus syrup or honey. But you can serve them as a supper dish with a savoury topping.

8 oz (225 g) flour
3 teaspoons baking powder   ½ teaspoon salt
1 tablespoon caster sugar (omit if using a savoury topping)
2 eggs, size 3, separated
12 fl oz (350 ml) milk
3 oz (75 g) margarine, melted

Preheat the waffle iron.
1. Sift together the dry ingredients. Beat the egg yolks with the milk, stir in the melted fat and stir into the dry ingredients.
2. Whisk the egg whites to stiff peaks and stir a heaped tablespoonful into the batter to lighten it, then scrape the batter on top of the egg whites and gently cut and fold together.
3. Bake, following directions for your waffle iron.

VARIATIONS

Raisin Waffles: add 2 oz (50 g) raisins or sultanas to the batter before folding in the egg whites.
Coconut Waffles: add 2 heaped tablespoons of desiccated coconut to the batter before folding in the egg whites.
Lemon Waffles: substitute 2 fl oz (50 ml) lemon juice for an equal quantity of milk.

Gauffres Bruxellois

Makes 6

These waffles are thin, crisp and extremely rich. They may be slightly soft as you take them from the iron, but will become crisp in a few seconds. Serve them either with caster sugar and a squeeze of lemon juice, or with soft vanilla ice-cream, or with soured cream and soft brown sugar as a sweet snack or pudding. *Do not butter* – they are so rich that they do not need it.

7 oz (200 g) flour
pinch of salt
2 oz (50 ml) salad oil
12 fl oz (350 ml) lager or light ale
grated rind of 1 lemon
½ teaspoon lemon juice
1 egg, size 1 or 2, or 2 eggs, size 3 or 4
½ teaspoon vanilla essence

1. Sift the flour and salt into a large bowl. Whisk together the oil, beer, lemon rind and juice, and the egg and stir into the dry ingredients. Add the vanilla essence. Cover and let the batter stand for at least 2 hours, or overnight in the refrigerator.

2. Preheat the waffle iron. Stir the batter lightly and pour into a jug. Pour sparingly on to the waffle iron (the batter is thin), and bake. Remove to rack and keep warm until all the waffles are made.

Cheese Waffles

Makes 8

Serve these subtly-flavoured crisp waffles with any creamed savoury mixture, or spread with softened butter and eat as a snack.

6 oz (175 g) flour
2 teaspoons baking powder
½ teaspoon bicarbonate of soda
½ teaspoon salt
good pinch of cayenne
3 eggs, size 3, separated
5 fl oz (150 ml) soured cream
6 fl oz (175 ml) milk
3 oz (75 g) margarine, melted
2 oz (50 g) strong Cheddar cheese, grated

Preheat the waffle iron.
1. Sift the dry ingredients into a large bowl. Beat the egg yolks with the soured cream and the milk. Add the liquid to the dry ingredients alternately with the melted margarine. Stir until the batter is just smooth, then mix in the cheese.
2. Whisk the egg whites to stiff peaks and stir 2 heaped tablespoons into the cheese batter to lighten it. Then scrape the batter on top of the egg whites and gently fold together.
3. Bake, and keep waffles warm on a rack until all are cooked.

Soured Milk Waffles

Makes about 7

I think these are my favourite waffles: deliciously rich, crisp and very light – a good foil for something like creamed chicken. The original recipe, from Wisconsin (the Dairy State), uses buttermilk, but as this can be hard to come by in certain parts of Britain, I make them very successfully with freshly soured milk.

3 eggs, size 3, separated
12 fl oz (350 ml) buttermilk or soured milk (to sour milk: stir 3
tablespoons of lemon juice into the milk and let it stand for 5 minutes)
2 oz (50 g) melted butter or margarine
6 oz (175 g) flour
2 oz (50 g) cornflour
2 teaspoons baking powder
½ teaspoon bicarbonate of soda
½ teaspoon salt
1 tablespoon caster sugar (optional; omit if using waffles for
a savoury dish)

Preheat the waffle iron.
1. Whisk the egg yolks, milk and melted fat together. Sift the dry ingredients into the liquid and stir well but do not over-beat.
2. Whisk the egg-whites until stiff. Stir 2 heaped tablespoons into the batter to lighten it, then scrape the batter on to the egg whites and fold together.
3. Bake, and serve for breakfast with honey or pancake syrup (page 93) or as a supper dish with any of the toppings on pages 64 and 70.

Potato Waffles

Makes 4

These waffles are crisp outside and meltingly soft inside – very good with a poached or fried egg on top, or with creamed vegetables. They freeze well.

12 oz (350 g) hot mashed potatoes
4 fl oz (100 ml) hot milk
3 tablespoons flour
1 oz (25 g) margarine or butter, melted
½ teaspoon salt
freshly ground black pepper
1 egg, beaten
1 heaped tablespoon finely chopped chives (optional)

1. Over a low heat, stir together the potatoes, milk, flour and margarine. Remove from the heat, season and beat in the egg. Add the chives, if using.
2. Bake as for any waffle – but allowing a few more minutes' baking time. Keep warm on a rack until all are cooked. They may be cooled and reheated in a hot oven or under a moderate grill when needed.

Rice Waffles

Makes about 6

For breakfast or brunch – delicately sweet waffles with an interesting texture. No one ever guesses that they are made with rice.

7 oz (200 g) flour
4 teaspoons baking powder
2 tablespoons caster sugar
½ teaspoon salt
4 oz (100 g) cold cooked rice
12 fl oz (350 ml) milk
1 egg, size 3, separated
1 oz (25 g) butter or margarine, melted

Preheat the waffle iron.
1. Sift the dry ingredients together, and mix in the rice with your fingers. Beat the milk with the egg yolk and melted butter or margarine and stir into the dry ingredients.
2. Whisk the egg whites to stiff peaks in a large bowl. Stir 2 heaped tablespoons into the batter and mix well, then scrape the batter on to the egg white and fold together.
3. Spoon the batter into the waffle iron, spreading it slightly. Do not over-fill, as this waffle is very light and puffy. Bake, and serve with melted butter. It is sweet enough not to need sugar or syrup for serving.

Ginger Waffles

Makes 6

These waffles are dense and rich-flavoured. They can be eaten with butter, cream or ice-cream, or on their own – like a sweet ginger biscuit.

6 oz (175 g) flour
3 teaspoons baking powder
½ teaspoon salt
1 teaspoon powdered ginger
3 eggs, separated
4 fl oz (100 ml) milk
3 fl oz (75 ml) oil
1 tablespoon black treacle
2 tablespoons golden syrup
1 oz (25 g) chopped ginger (candied, or in syrup)

Preheat the waffle iron.
1. Sift the dry ingredients together. In a large bowl, whisk the egg whites to soft peaks. Without washing the beater, whisk the egg yolks, milk and oil together, then beat in the black treacle, syrup and chopped ginger. Lightly stir into the dry ingredients. Mix 2 heaped tablespoons of egg white into the batter to lighten it, then scrape the batter on top of the egg whites and gently fold together.
2. Spoon this (thick) batter on to the waffle iron, spreading it out. Bake, and keep warm on a rack until all are cooked. Serve with butter for breakfast – or as a dessert, with vanilla ice-cream or stiffly whipped cream.

Butternut Waffles

Makes 6

These waffles are sweet and crunchy, and make a pleasant and simple dessert served with whipped cream, or soured cream or ice-cream. They freeze well.

6 oz (175 g) flour
2½ teaspoons baking powder
good pinch of salt
3 tablespoons soft brown sugar
2 eggs, size 3, separated
10 fl oz (275 ml) milk
2 fl oz (50 ml) oil
3 oz (75 g) coarsely chopped walnuts

Preheat the waffle iron.
1. Sift together the flour, baking powder and salt and thoroughly mix in the brown sugar. Whisk the egg whites until stiff in a large bowl. Without washing the whisk, beat the egg yolks, milk and oil together. Stir into the dry ingredients (taking care not to over-beat) and mix in the nuts.
2. Stir 2 tablespoons of the egg whites into the batter and mix well, then scrape the batter on top of the egg whites and gently fold together.
3. Bake, and either keep warm on a rack in a cool oven, or cool and toast at serving time.

Crisp Chocolate Waffles

Makes 6

Cut in small portions, these waffles make the most delicious crisp chocolate biscuits which can be stored in an airtight tin for weeks. They can be
reheated carefully under a grill, but they catch easily. Delicious served
with sweetened whipped cream or ice-cream.

5 oz (150 g) flour
2 oz (50 g) cornflour
2 teaspoons baking powder
good pinch of salt
7 oz (200 g) caster sugar
1 oz (25 g) butter or margarine
1½ oz (40 g) cocoa powder
2 heaped teaspoons instant coffee powder
2 eggs, size 3
3 fl oz (75 ml) vegetable oil
½–1 teaspoon vanilla essence
4–5 fl oz (100–150 ml) milk

Preheat the waffle iron.
1. Sift together the flour, cornflour, baking powder and salt, and mix
well with the sugar. Heat the butter or margarine with the cocoa powder
and coffee and mix well. Beat the eggs with the oil, vanilla essence and
milk and gradually stir into the dry ingredients, then add the cocoa mixture. Do not over-mix – any small lumps will smooth out in the baking.
2. Bake on moderate heat, and remove. The waffle will be limp and floppy,
but will crisp up on a cake rack within about 10–15 minutes.

Hazelnut Wholewheat Waffles

Makes 7

Serve these waffles with whipped butter (page 92), golden syrup, or orange sugar – made from 1 teaspoon grated orange rind stirred into 3 oz (75 g) caster sugar – which has a pleasant affinity with any nut waffle or cake.

4 oz (100 g) wholewheat flour
4 oz (100 g) white flour
2 teaspoons baking powder
½ teaspoon salt
3 eggs, size 3, separated
12 fl oz (350 ml) milk
2 oz (50 g) margarine, melted
2 oz (50 g) hazelnuts, coarsely chopped

Preheat the waffle iron.

1. Sift the flours with the baking powder and salt. Whisk the egg yolks with the milk and melted margarine and stir into the dry ingredients, then add the nuts. Do not over-beat!

2. In a large bowl, whisk the egg whites until stiff and stir about 2 heaped tablespoons into the batter to lighten it. Scrape the batter on to the egg whites, lightly fold together and bake.

Pineapple Waffles

Makes about 8

These waffles are quite sweet. Serve them simply with a trickle of melted butter and some icing sugar. They reheat well and can be frozen.

3 eggs, size 3, separated
3 oz (75 g) margarine, melted
9 fl oz (250 ml) milk
12 oz (350 g) tin crushed pineapple
7 oz (200 g) flour
2 teaspoons baking powder
½ teaspoon salt
1 tablespoon caster sugar

Preheat the waffle iron.
1. Whisk the egg yolks with the melted margarine, milk and 3 fl oz (75 ml) pineapple juice (drained from the tin of crushed fruit). Sift the dry ingredients into the liquid, and mix well. Stir in the pineapple.
2. In a large bowl, whisk the egg whites to stiff peaks, and stir 2 heaped tablespoons into the batter to lighten it. Scrape the batter on to the remaining egg whites, and carefully cut and fold together.
3. Spread the batter on the waffle iron but do not over-fill. Bake for a minute or two less than for standard crisp waffles as this version can burn rather easily.

Margaret Smythe's Homemade Orange Liqueur

This liqueur can be kept topped up with more of everything for ever – the taste will vary somewhat, but it is always useful for making any crêpes that call for an orange liqueur, and is much less costly than luxury liqueurs.

2 large bright-skinned oranges
6 oz (175 g) caster sugar
25 fl oz (700 ml) gin or vodka
a litre-size bottle

Thinly peel the oranges and finely shred the rind. Put the rind in the bottle. Squeeze the juice and mix it with the sugar. Pour it into the bottle and shake well. Add the gin or vodka, cork, and let it stand for 2 months. Strain off whatever you want to use.

Whipped Butter

An American delicacy often served with pancakes and waffles. In the United States and Canada, whipped butter is sold in supermarkets, but it has not yet appeared in the shops in Britain.

8 oz (225 g) unsalted butter
4 fl oz (100 ml) double or whipping cream

Put the butter and cream into a large bowl and whisk together until all the cream is absorbed and the mixture is fluffy. Cover tightly and refrigerate.

Honey Butter

Serve cold or heat up very carefully to pour on pancakes and waffles. Again, this is a transatlantic delight, often discovered with pleasure by visitors to North America.

6 oz (175 g) clear honey
4 oz (100 g) butter, at room temperature

Add the honey slowly to the softened butter and beat with a fork. When blended, cover and refrigerate.

Pancake and Waffle Syrup

Makes about 8 fl oz (225 ml) syrup

This recipe is called Mock Maple Syrup in old American cookery books. It comes from thrift-conscious New England, and makes a rich-flavoured alternative to good old golden syrup. Nice on ice-cream too.

6 oz (175 g) light brown sugar
3 fl oz (75 ml) water
pinch of salt
½ teaspoon vanilla essence

In a small heavy saucepan, stir the sugar into the water and add the salt and vanilla. Bring to the boil, then simmer for about 2 minutes. Serve cold.

INDEX